Our ~~NO FAIL~~ Pretty-Damn-Reliable Method to Start Kicking Ass with Container Soy Candle Making

by

Lisa Lively, Aggie's LLC

Tired of heat guns, sinkholes, wet spots, and other things that totally piss you off when making container soy candles? Here's my step-by-step single-pour method including specific supplies & recipes we currently use in our own business so you can get started immediately with your own success!

Contents

Introduction

I am so honored that you've spent money to purchase this book! I'm even more honored that you're now spending your precious time reading it. With that in mind I've made every effort to make this a great resource tool for you. I realize the title of this book sounds a little sassy and unprofessional, but if you've experienced the frustrations I have with making soy candles I bet you'll keep reading! Let's just say you have to keep your humor or you'll go crazy here.

First things first - You might notice that the formatting of this book is a little hinky; so, if you're actually reading this I must have managed to push enough buttons to get it published! I hope we can laugh about the editing flaws and just focus on leaving you satisfied as a consumer and that both your money and time were well spent here. A book publisher/editor I'm clearly not! Next to making soy candles I can not remember something so frustrating to figure out besides book publishing!

The basis of this book comes from my belief that the more we share with each other, the more we all succeed. I come from a small town in Eastern Oregon and when we were running our cute little bungalow boutique (back in the day) this "the more we share, the more we all succeed" idea was my mantra.

When others were pondering about business ideas for our town I often encouraged them to view the other existing businesses as a compliment and an asset to their own potential business rather than a threat or competition. What I meant by this was simple and I understand it's not necessarily applicable across the board. However, in a small town relying on drawing in tourism to add to the economy it's hard to argue from a visitor's perspective. My point was this: the more we have here in our little town, the more reasons people have to come, stay, and spend their money. There really is room for two espresso machines folks!

Fast forward a few years after a stink in the economy and a desire to keep pursuing my own business and that's when I decided a product-based business was a viable option for us. My goal was to create our own candle line for our little bungalow boutique and eventually wholesale this line here in the Pacific Northwest. Long story short - we did it!

The most challenging part, however, was a serious lack of credible information available through all the normal channels when one decides to learn a new skill (i.e. Google)(quit laughing, I know I'm not the only one who'd be lost without Google).

I found that people were very guarded with their "secrets" and not inclined to help you learn your way around in the soy candle making business. We persisted, though, and went forward to create a business that has exceeded our expectations. I think it's silly that anyone has "secrets" in this business. Next to prostitution it's probably the oldest profession there is! So, it's my desire to share some "secrets" here with you.

Before we get into the book itself let me stress that I'm not claiming to be the be-all end-all here in candle making; however,

I do have a few things I can claim in my favor: decent writing skills, a notebook documenting my own years of trial and error in candle-making, and a determination that is often both my best and worst asset.

My hope with this book is to reach the small business entrepreneur, hobbyist, fundraiser, or crafter seeking to develop and possibly improve their skills in candle making to a point that they can consider pursuing the craft for profit. If I don't cover what you think should be covered, I'm certainly open to suggestions and ideas that will help make this a better resource in the future and I welcome your feedback and suggestions. So, for the benefit of all, please share!

If you decide to leave a review please consider the intention behind this effort; I'm not an author by trade and sincerely just want to help others succeed. Please don't ding me on the formatting! (or grammar for that matter, pretty please!)

Lastly, I wish you all the success you desire and are seeking. I may have been in your shoes at one point or another and I hope this book leads you towards your own victories. I'm passionate about small business success and I'd love to hear from you!

You can reach out to me through our contact page on our website at www.aggiesonmain.com. I'd seriously be tickled to hear from you!

Our ~~NO FAIL~~ Pretty-Damn-Reliable Method to Start Kicking Ass with Container Soy Candle Making

Chapter 1: Who this book is for: Beginners, Intermediate Learners, Budding Entrepreneurs, Fundraisers, and Crafters

Beginners & Intermediate Learners!
This is a great starting point to get a good foundation under you. I share specifics on supplies, processes, and even "recipes" we currently use in our own business so that you have an opportunity to grow and learn without being overwhelmed with the massive amount of information (and sadly, misinformation) that exists out there. The reality is that candle making has been around for many years, but soy container candle making is relatively new. There's just not as much soy-specific information out there and what is out there is often a hodge-podge of misinformation and old wives tales. It's discouraging, really.

TIP: Start here with this book and get a foundation under you. Then use it as a jumping off point for your own creativity! Then send me an email and let me know what kind of trouble you're stirring up as a result!

Budding Entrepreneurs!
Looking to start a business and make some extra money? This is a low-cost, low-risk way of trying out your hand at candle making. With this step-by-step guide and complete equipment list I take out the guesswork that often leads to money down the drain (ask me how I know!). I give you solid information that I've already tested with the help and assistance of the manufacturers and suppliers I use so that you can go forward and get right to work. This is a great business that satisfies the creativity bug some people have, but is also scaleable, too, depending on your own needs and desires for your business. I love cheering on small businesses, so you'll have to be sure to connect with me so I can marvel at your successes you're bound to achieve!

Fundraisers!
Fundraisers are often product-based and this is a great way to explore the possibility of doing soy container candles for your group. The specific recipes, detailed list of supplies, and lengthy directions are a perfect place to start so that you can quickly evaluate this opportunity and see if it pencils out for your group.

Crafters!
Just like being creative and interested in learning about container soy candle making? This is a great place to start mainly for the detailed instructions and the specific recipes. Be assured you can follow my recipes and produce results that will be perfect for gift-giving or for whatever you choose and it will require very minimal expenditure to achieve these great results. I

can't tell you how much wax, oil, etc. I have wasted just because I had to find my own starting point when I was first learning about container soy candles.

Chapter 2: What you'll find in this book: Detailed Instructions for Soy Container Candle Making, My Mistakes, Troubleshooting Guide, Resources to grow your business, and Specific Candle Recipes!

TIP: What you'll find in this book is basically what I wish someone would have told me when I was first starting out in soy container candle making. Additionally, you'll also find the following:

1. Instructions using specific equipment and supplies (including links where applicable) to make container soy candles. If you're reading this I bet you're already aware of the many different types of candles and that each has its own process, components, testing requirements, and end results. So, just to be clear, this book is only about soy container candle making. The testing I've done, trouble-shooting, etc. is all based on soy container candles. Did I mention this is about soy container candles?

2. My mistakes! I've included many of the costly mistakes we've personally made in our own candle-making journey and how you can avoid them and save some money in the process! Look for the Troubleshooting section in Chapter 22 for all the details;

3. A resource section where you can find all of the supplies and equipment that I personally use in our business and have had good success with. I'm including specific links to the tools, equipment, supplies, components, and resource information throughout the book that I personally use to create our products that we sell wholesale throughout the Pacific Northwest as well as on our website (www.aggiesonmain.com) (shameless plug?)(you bet!)

4. Specific "recipes" - yep, I'm seriously going to share some of my personal recipes for products that we have manufactured and sold in our own business. I promise to walk you through some of our own tried and true recipes that we have tested and ultimately sold (successfully and profitably) through our business;

5. A summary of links and resources in the very back of the book. If you're like me and you know it all and just need the meat - I get it. It's there for that reason and more power to you. Get going!

6. TIPS galore! Throughout this book I include a number of TIPS (all unpredictable formatting aside) Just look for "TIPS" in all caps. My TIPS are little gems that have often made all the difference in the quality of our final product. Some TIPS are big, some are more like little information nuggets, but I promise they all have a place in your candle making adventure.

7. A way to connect with me if you have additional questions! As

a first-time "author" (I'm laughing as I write that) I will have surely overlooked something, so please feel free to reach out to me and I'll be happy to help. Seriously. If you've invested your time, energy and money into this "book" then I want to offer support afterwards if you need it. I may or may not have all the answers for any issues you may run into, but get in touch and we'll go from there!

Again, please keep in mind I'm writing this for a beginner to intermediate learner interested in container soy candle making. If you're advanced in your learning this may not be for you and I suspect you have something to teach all of us. (please be kind in your review!)(and, hey! I'd love to hear from you so I can improve this book!)

Chapter 3: What's NOT in here: Anything unrelated to Soy Container Candle Making

I'll keep this short and sweet. This is about making container soy candles only as that is my specialty. To be honest, I have zero experience working with paraffin candles! I will not discuss anything besides natural soy wax candles that are made in some form of container. I will not cover anything paraffin-related, no votives or pillars requiring a mold, no gel candles, etc. This is strictly a container soy candle resource as that is where my experience and background lies. Thanks in advance for understanding!

There is an enormous amount of information out there about candle making in general and some of it is useful in making soy container candles. However, be very careful of using information about making paraffin candles or paraffin/soy blend candles though as it does not necessarily apply to candle making using all-natural soy wax.

This book is intended to be a tool for you if you're just starting out. I SO wish I had had something like this when I first started! I can't tell you how many websites, forums, books, and just plain old trial and error I suffered through while trying to learn this craft. My pocketbook suffered even more!

Chapter 4: Soy Candles & The Benefits of Soy Wax

Soy wax is a vegetable wax made from the oil of soybeans. Some of the reasons we chose this wax for our own business include the fact that soy is not a petroleum by-product. We also liked the idea that we could get our hands on a USA-grown product in the larger quantities that we needed to support the growth of our business. Plus, it cleans up with soap and water and is 100% biodegradable!

Additional benefits include:
Soy wax is an all-natural product from a renewable resource made from U.S. grown soy beans which supports U.S. agriculture as well as the U.S. economy. What's not to like?

Soy produces a cleaner burn than paraffin and does not release toxins into the air when burned. It's less likely to trigger allergies, too! (Keep in mind, however, any candle can produce soot when burning if it is not wicked properly or if it's burned too long)

Some believe that soy candles burn up to 50% longer, but I think that's debatable with a pure soy wax candle with no additives. I haven't seen this in my own candle testing either. If a candle was created with a blend of waxes to create a harder wax, I expect you may lengthen the time the candle can burn, but this would require significant experimenting and testing. I'm not convinced, but I certainly could be wrong here.

Chapter 5: Choosing the Right Soy Wax for your Project

There are so many options when looking for a soy wax to make candles with. There are soy waxes specifically for making pillar candles, melting tarts, votives, containers, and probably some I'm not even aware of. We use one soy wax product to produce our container candles (I'll share more about that in a bit!) and a different soy wax product to produce our Soy Melting Tarts. If you're interested in the wax melting tarts, contact me and I'll fill you in!

Also, be careful in choosing your wax as some "Soy Wax" might actually be a blend of soy and paraffin (often done to achieve a better scent throw and glass adhesion). If a pure soy product is important to you, just be aware you have to read labels and ask questions sometimes to be sure of what you're getting. Kind of like food labels with less regulation.

You'll learn quickly with wax, just like everything else in candle making, that what one person loves another person might seriously despise. (and for a variety of reasons to boot!)

TIP: Decide on the type of container you want to use first and then choose your wax. Some waxes are easier to work with in small containers and some are easier to work with in larger containers (and it's just as accurate to say some containers are easier to make into candles than others) Some waxes are less expensive, but perfectly suitable for a small travel tin. Some are more expensive or contain additional additives to help it perform better and are easier to use in larger containers.

In our business we use C-3 Nature Wax (I purchase this from www.cierracandles.com) manufactured by Elevance Renewable Sciences and one of the main reasons I like this wax is because I can call or email Elevance directly and get help with specific problems I've had while learning to use the product. I also like it because it's a high-quality wax that holds a solid fragrance load (6-10%) without significant problems and includes natural antioxidants to aid in stabilizing the wax and preventing discoloration when using certain oils. It's really a few steps above the standard craft store wax which is often the same product that is sold to the commercial bread making industry as shortening! I bet you were dying to know that.

TIP: All waxes sold for candle making indicate the wax's ability to hold a certain fragrance oil "load". This is usually indicated as a certain percentage. For example if you're using the GB464 Wax available at www.CandleScience.com you'll see that they've listed a 12% maximum load for this wax. That means if you have 30 ounces of wax you can use up to 3.6 ounces of oil (30 oz x .12 = 3.6 oz).

Chapter 6: Choosing Wicks

Good news! All wicks made in the USA are lead-free. You may see zinc-core wicks and they're purportedly safe, but I have my doubts. I have burned a certain big-named candle in the past and always thought it smelled metallic when burning and it turned out to have a zinc core. When I investigated further I found that the company used zinc-core wicks for rigidity. There are better choices for you, though!

Choosing a wick is a critical part of the process and you really need to understand how to choose wicks based on your container, type of wax, fragrance load, and any additives you might use.

Let me be clear and blunt here: sadly there's no magic, easy answer. When it comes to wicks there are an (almost) infinite number of choices! Add to that an infinite number of container choices, a variety of waxes and fragrance oils and even I can see how boggling the math gets from here.

So, where do you start? After you have selected a container and a wax I would look first to the wax manufacturer and/or supplier to see if they recommend any wicks in particular. Most suppliers even have wick selection guides (like this one here) (www.candlescience.com/learning/wick-guide) based on the container size and type of wax you're using. Select the "series" of wicks recommended for what wax and container you've chosen.

By "series" I mean the name of the group of wicks your particular supplier carries and possibly recommends for your situation. For example, we currently use the "Eco Series" wicks in most of our candles. You can see them at www.CandleScience.com online. They have a number of wick series' including the HTP, LX and CSN. In our early days of learning we actually tested all of these wicks and ended up preferring the Eco series for the wax we were using.

So, back to the wick selection. Pick a "series" that is recommended for your particular wax/container combo and then get a few sizes within that series to test. The supplier or their Wick Selection Guide will likely recommend a series and possibly even a size to start with, but it's up to you to do the actual testing. In other words, the recommendation they may give you in the Wick Selection Guide is just a starting point. Get a size bigger and a size smaller along with the size recommended and you're set to start testing.

You absolutely have to do your own testing to determine what's safe and appropriate for your individual variables.

TIP: Do not, for the safety of your end user, skip doing your own testing. You can find detailed information on test burning in Chapter 19 if you need to skip ahead!

The wicks I like and why I like them: I've tested a number of wicks and the Eco Series is holding my attention right now. Whenever I test a new container/wax/oil formulation I test with the Eco series as well as the CD series. People rave about the CD series and I do agree they are a good option for use in soy wax, but Eco just seems to edge them out every time. The one thing I like about the Eco wicks is that when I go to trim my candles each time I light them there's enough of the wick available to grab hold of and just pinch with my finger without removing so much of the wick it has trouble burning anymore afterwards. The CD wicks have been more delicate in this regard for me. Just my experience for what it's worth. Again, please do your own testing and see what you experience AND what you prefer for your own project!

TIP: Do yourself a favor and take good notes! I promise you won't be sorry. Take the kind of notes that you'll be able to decipher a year from now if you need to (and you may). Your notes will pay off and will be helpful to you if they include information such as the date, time, weather, containers, wicks, wax, oils, room temperature, etc. Basically, any variables you can make note of will help you document your successes and give you some insight to recreate those successes in the future.

TIP: I would encourage you to test only a few wicks at a time and keep clear notes on the results and performance. Testing too many at one time will only leave you confused and unclear of what to do next.

Chapter 7: Fragrance Oils Vs. Essential Oils

This particular topic could be a book all on its own! So, please bear with me here. This explanation is way oversimplified, but the main difference is that essential oils are naturally occurring substances while fragrance oils are manufactured artificially.

Essential oils are actual essences extracted from plants and all of their little parts and pieces (seeds, leaves, stems, etc) through distillation and/or expression. Again, this is oversimplified, but you get the gist.

Fragrance oils are synthetic compounds that are manufactured artificially to mimic the scents of natural essential oils. Many fragrance oils are manufactured using some essential oils as components in the manufacturing process, but they also include chemical compounds, too, to help them function safely and properly in various applications such as candle making.

TIP: when selecting fragrance oils take time to seek out quality oils. We prefer oils that are "Phthalate Free". Phthalates are nasty chemicals used in making plastic goods soft and pliable. (ever heard of "vegan leather"?) I would encourage you to seek out information regarding the use of this chemical so that you can make your own informed decision on whether it fits in your own project/business needs and goals.

Essential oils are generally more expensive than fragrance oils and not as likely to be used for candle making just because the cost is often prohibitive. I'm certainly not an expert on essential oils, but would encourage you to research this thoroughly if you decide you really want to pursue candle making with pure essential oils. There seems to be very limited credible information available and I suspect it's a matter of testing on your own to know for sure if something will work safely and reliably for your intended purpose.

For our candle business we have a classic lavender fragrance oil that we use from www.CandleScience.com (specific link listed in the resource section), but we have also experimented with using pure lavender essential oil from www.EssentialWholesale.com and we absolutely fell head over heels for the pure essential oil candle. Sadly, it just didn't pencil out for us to make them and sell them at the price point we needed them to come in at. Bummer!

This has clearly been a very basic description of the difference between Essential Oils and Fragrance Oils. It's not in any way intended to be your sole source of information; however, the following is a great place to start if you want to learn more:

For more in depth information on Essential Oils please see the National Association for Holistic Aromatherapy (www.naha.org) for some great information on what nature has to offer us!

For a more in depth description about Fragrance Oils please see: Candle Science What's in a Fragrance Oil?

Chapter 8: Choosing Containers

When choosing containers keep this in mind always: heat resistant glass or ceramic is critical for producing a safe product. Please consider safety first when choosing the containers for your creations. So many people are making candles in darling, delicate little tea cups and other antique vessels, but I'm not always convinced that these are a good choice.

TIP: If we're being honest, those cute little tea cups were just not meant to house a flame, folks. It's good fun to make candles out of repurposed containers, but always keep safety a priority.

Some of my favorite containers are those little mason jars. You can find them all over the place, but www.CierraCandles.com has been a great supplier for us since we live on the West coast. You can check out their mason jars (and other containers) at www.cierracandles.com.

There are plenty of sources online for containers that are well-suited for candle making. Our favorites include SKS Bottle & Packaging as well as Candle Science. Both places offer a great selection of containers at great prices and the shipping is fair. (free shipping at this time on SKS Bottle & Packaging if you spend over $250)

Chapter 9: Candle Making Equipment (all the nuts and bolts that will get the job done)

We've been talking supplies, but what about the actual equipment you'll need to make your candles? This includes everything from Presto Pots to stir sticks and everything in between. Just a note about the equipment list. It's just like everything else - everyone has their favorite equipment to use. Find what works best for you and go with it.

I promised details in here, though, so here's what we'll talk about in this section:

Notebook & Pen (I know, kind of goes without saying!)
Calculator (nothing fancy, just basic math functions)
Digital scale
Thermometer (digital is great!)
Wooden spoons or paint stir sticks
Wax melters (I'll detail a couple of options)
Straws (yep, drinking straws)
Aluminum pouring pots (or other pourable containers)
Wick holders
High temperature hot glue pot & glue pellets (plus other options)
Paper towels
Trays (optional)
Bun Rack (optional)

Notebook/Pen

Don't mind me, I'm just going to reiterate the importance of note-taking here...again! I promise you won't regret it. I would encourage you to write in a way that someone else will be able to pick up your notes a year from now and decipher with some degree of clarity what you've written and documented about your own process. When I first started I made all sorts of scribbles and notes thinking I would know what I meant, but even when I returned to my notes a week later (or sometimes the following day) I was confused about what I had written. I'll bet you're ahead of the game here, but just know I've made some of the most ridiculous mistakes in my enthusiasm and this is one of them!

Calculator
I have a simple pocket-sized, solar-powered Sharp calculator that I used when I did piece work for a fishing lure company over 20+ years ago. All you need is to be able to determine percentages and a basic plus and minus feature. You can protect it from wax and oil spills by placing it inside of a plastic bag while it's in your work space.

Digital Scale
There are so many choices for scales. You don't have to use the exact scale we use to achieve good results. At a minimum I would recommend one that reads out in grams, ounces, and pounds. I have used all three of these settings on my scale at one point or another. This is the scale we currently use: Ozeri Scale. Honestly, what I've liked most about the scale we use now is that it's completely flat on the surface (all the controls are on the side of the scale) I slip it inside of a plastic bag to protect

it from wax and oil spills and it works great! There are tons of scales in the $20 range that will work great. Don't feel like you have to put out a ton of money for something like this. Make sure the surface you have it on is solid and level and you should have an accurate reading every time you use it.

TIP: I encourage you to use a scale to measure your wax and fragrance oils in ounces. The details really do matter and accuracy will be your friend if you're looking for consistent, reliable, reproducible results in candle-making. Skip measuring your oils with measuring spoons!

Wooden Spoons/Paint Stir Sticks
This sounds silly to even mention this, but I promised details! My favorite tool to stir my candle wax with right now is a stir stick from the local paint department. They're like a miniature paddle, cheap, and last forever. Some people prefer a more refined tool such as a wooden spoon. Just use something that is comfortable to you and does the job.

Thermometer
Depending on what size of a candle you're making and/or what type of container you're pouring into as well as what kind of wax and oil you're using you'll want a quick, reliable way to monitor the temperature of the wax. There are all sorts of devices to do this (and probably an app for that for all I know). What I like is a simple meat thermometer that reads off a digital number. I purchased mine through CandleScience several years ago and I still use the same one today. (See one similar here) I like it because it was fairly inexpensive, includes an alert/timer

function, includes a clip so you can hook it on the side of your pouring pitcher, and generally does the job without bother. Because, who needs a bother?

Wax Melters
There are a couple of options I think are safe and suitable for someone learning this craft and/or looking to grow a business or hobby. The Presto Pot is my preference for hobby candle making. Make sure you get one that has a temperature control unit. It can melt up to about 4 pounds of wax safely, but please be vigilant when using such an appliance and never leave it unattended when you're melting your wax.

I have tried the double-boiler method for melting wax, but I was just not a fan. Wax and water are not friends and I'll just end the discussion there.

If you're looking to upgrade and want to take your candle making to the next level here's the melter we currently use (we call her Penny): Primo 100 from Waxmelters. They have a variety of sizes and you might be surprised at what you can get in the way of a professional melter for the money. It might seem like a frivolous expense when first starting out, but I like how safe it is to operate. We work with 50-100 pounds of hot wax at a time at very high temperatures and I'm confident in our safety with this unit.

TIP: A great piece of advice I got when we purchased Penny was that you'll outgrow your tank sooner than you think. So, if you think a 50 pound capacity melter will work for you, you might be better off to go ahead and buy a 75 pound capacity melter instead. Plan for your success in advance, right? We've never been sorry we purchased the 100 pound capacity melter. In fact, we didn't have it very long when we decided to buy another!

Straws (or other hollow, sturdy tube)
This one is a crack up, I know. My favorite candle-making hack has, by far, been the use of a straw to do wick placements in the containers. You slip the wick assembly (wicking with the metal clip attached) into the straw, dip the metal clip into your hot glue and then center the wick in your container. Once you have the wick centered and set you just pull your straw out and you're ready for the next one!

TIP: I'm here to officially tell you that you DO NOT need fancy wick setting devices. I have two in my basement if you are a glutton for punishment. Straws will do. So will old ink pens with the guts removed. I'd love to send you to the link that shows the wick setters we bought for our business, but I think those people probably spent a small fortune developing their device and honestly there probably are people that swear by them. My experience with the device was that you really had to have just the right size of container or it slipped around and was difficult to keep centered anyway.

Aluminum Pouring Pots
I'm recommending aluminum pouring pots (I get mine from Candle Science here) because they're light and sturdy. They're also cheap and easy to find. It's a great container that's easy to control (unless you get sassy and try to fill it too full). I've seen

other people use glass measuring containers and I think that's fine, but they're heavy! Improvise with what works for you here.

TIP: You don't need a separate pouring pitcher for every scent you have. I'll save myself the embarrassment and just tell you to get two or three at the most to start. I bet that will suffice and you'll know if you need more than that. (I have about 30 in my stash if you need one!) With our method we'll have you pouring your wax at a higher temperature so you won't have a bunch of wax filled pitchers waiting around until they cool to a certain temperature. Who has time for that?

Wick Holders
Again, so many options! I suggest trying what you might already have on hand. Old clothespins work perfectly if your container isn't too big. I prefer the standard metal wick bars through Candle Science (available through most suppliers in some variation or other). I like the wick bars because they're easy to store, use, and I'm just used to using them. I suspect if I had started with clothespins, those would be my preference today. Just play around and see what you like!

High Temperature Glue Pot & Pellets
Again, a number of choices here to secure wicks in your containers. In our early days of learning we tried the little stick-um pads that you can buy from most any candle supply company or craft store (see an example here) and we've tried the average craft-store glue pot and pellets that are available through said average craft store. Both are just okay and may be just fine for you if you're doing a small project.

Where I feel like we really hit our stride was when I obtained a 7" Variable Temperature Craft Skillet and Diamond Cubes Skillet Glue from Commercial Hot Glue (a Merchant General Corporation). What I like about this is that the glue is a "high-melt" glue; so, if I choose to pour 175 degree wax into a container I don't have to worry about the wick coming loose (because it may otherwise melt the glue holding the wick in place) in the container.

I also like that the skillet is large enough to have two people using it at the same time and it keeps up with our production. The skillet also has a variable temperature that we often adjust up or down depending on how much glue we have in the skillet. It's a keeper. With all that said, there are truly a number of options to secure your wick in the container. You don't have to do exactly what I'm doing to achieve results. I promised specifics so pick and choose what's best for your adventure!

Paper Towels
These are just handy for spills or a quick wipe of a pitcher after you have poured a batch and want to ready it for the next one. I hate that I go through paper towels, but they do work and they do keep messes to a minimum.

Trays
These are simple sheet pan trays commonly used in bakeries (see a sample here). The half-size (about 13"x18") is the one we use daily. They're the perfect size to hold a batch of just about anything we make and they're not so big that you can't lift them

and move them around once they're loaded with a batch of candles.

Bun Rack

Okay, this is probably not necessary for the average hobbyist or fundraiser, but check this out! The bun rack we use can be seen here. We love, love, love it! It's a great space-saver if you're working in cramped quarters and I love being able to pour candles in one room, set them on the rack, and then move the rack into another room to clean and label everything.

TIP: If you decide to purchase a bun rack be sure to get the one that you can load from the narrow sides (referred to as an "end load") like this one here. This rack will accept the half-sheet size trays as well as the full-size trays if you prefer those. Just beware if you purchase the one like this (referred to as a "side load") your half-sheet size trays will be too small to even use. If you do make the mistake of getting the full-size sheet pans and the bun rack that only accepts that larger size pan your trays will end up so heavy with all of your candles loaded on them you won't be able to move them! Confused? Don't worry, it wasn't a deal breaker for us, but I promised details!

Chapter 10: Preparing Your Workspace (for something epic!)

Select a space you can dedicate to the task for at least a full day, preferably two. Your home's kitchen may fit the bill as long as you have enough level counter space or table space to work with. How much room do you need? You'll need an area for measuring out and melting the wax as well as an area to actually pour your candles. The space you need will depend on the number of candles you'll be pouring (plan for at least a few inches between candles when you pour them); so, just plan accordingly.

Don't have room in your kitchen? I've used a spare bedroom with saw horses and plywood cut in half lengthwise to provide a long, level surface. I especially like plywood and sawhorses (or small plastic shelf units in place of the sawhorses) because they are light and easy to set up and take down if you need to store them away when you need to use the space for other things.

Make sure your work surface is level and free from drafts. You may want to cover the work surface with butcher paper or newspaper just to make cleanup easy.

Keep in mind that fragrance oils do have the potential to damage surfaces; so, just be aware and plan accordingly. If you're concerned about this use something to cover your work surface that the oil can't penetrate while you're working. I love using giant parchment sheets! (link listed in resource section)

To avoid problems with sinkholes, wet spots, etc. it really helps to have a room where you can control the temperature for the duration of your task (including the cooling/setup time for the candles after they have been poured). Some containers (i.e. our current 8 ounce straight-sided jars) do well being poured in a moderately warm room (65-70 degrees) while other containers (i.e. our larger 16 ounce straight sided jars) do better in a cooler setting (50-60 degrees) and still other containers (i.e. our 4 ounce travel tins) are (for the most part) not fussy at all about room temperature.

It might go without saying, but prepare yourself for the task you are about to tackle. Draw yourself a road map first. Gather your equipment and supplies ahead of time. You'll save a ton of time, money, and headaches!

Chapter 11: Making Your Candles: Our ~~No Fail~~ Pretty-Damn-Reliable Single-Pour Method with Step-by-Step Instructions - PREP WORK

Fair warning, this is going to be a meaty few chapters! (Can I please ask one more time for you to overlook the horrible formatting that may or may not appear here?) (Can I also ask that you bear with me - I realize this could probably be organized better, too!)

What follows is the actual process/method we use in our business and have experienced a satisfying level of success with it. It's the process that we have used to grow our business significantly in the last few years. I've mentioned this before, but I have found that the details really matter with this craft. (who knew?) So, here's the nitty-gritty as promised:

PREP WORK
Set up your room (correct temperature, no drafts), and plenty of space to work. I usually make sure my room is about 60-70 degrees unless I'm pouring larger, fatter candles. Those do better if they cool faster, so I'll keep the room at 50-60 degrees give or take a few degrees when pouring those. For the 8 oz straight-sided jars and the 4 oz tins we use in our recipes in Chapter 23 a room that is 60-70 degrees works best.

Sit down and draw yourself a map of what you want to do. Determine what you're making, how many you're making, and how much wax, oil, and other supplies needed to complete the project.

Chapter 12: Calculating the Amount of Wax & Oil You Need

So, here's a handy online calculator tool you can use to start with: Candle Tech Wax Calculator. (If you are reading the traditional print version of this, just google "Candle Tech Wax Calculator) You just enter the weight of your empty container as well as the weight of the same container filled with water and the calculator does the rest. (if the link doesn't work try typing the words "candle tech wax calculator" into your search engine).

I would encourage you to use this as a general starting point as everyone has a different idea of how full they should fill a particular container. I also like to plan for a couple of extra ounces in a batch in case I accidentally overfill something (trust me on this). Also, depending on the size and shape of your container you may fill your candles to a different level than someone else might. I literally find my starting point and then dial it in from there depending on the containers I'm using, how much fragrance oil I'm using, how full I fill the containers, etc.

For the recipes in this book here's how I proceed with calculating the amount of oil needed:

When making candles it's common practice to use a percentage of the total amount of wax in your batch to determine the fragrance "load" or the amount of fragrance oil used. For example, if the total amount of wax you are using is 65 ounces and you are shooting to use a 6 percent fragrance load you simply determine what 6% of the 65 oz is:

65 oz x .06 = 3.9 oz

So, for this particular batch of candles you would use 3.9 oz of fragrance oil.

TIP: Another easy way to figure out how much wax you need is to place your container on a scale and tare it out so that the scale reads "0". Then take some water and pour it into the container until it is filled to where you think you want the fill line to be if you were actually pouring the wax. Record the weight of the water you just poured and this will be the weight of the wax you need for that container. Proceed and test this out as you'll still need to experiment a little bit depending on how full you want your containers to ultimately be.

TIP: Manufacturers and suppliers commonly list the "wax weight" or "fill weight" for containers, but you still need to do you own testing and measuring for this to see exactly what amount will be correct for your needs. You may prefer your jar more full or less full. See an example of this here.

TIP: When unsure I always err on the side of a little extra wax (maybe just an ounce or two) just to be sure I have enough to fill all the containers to the level I want them filled to. There's nothing more frustrating than to prepare, plan, and pay attention to all of these details than getting all the way to the end and be short one lousy ounce of wax when filling a container.

CALCULATING WAX & OIL EXAMPLE: If I want to prepare a batch of four (4) 8 oz straight-sided jars here's what my notes look like:

First I calculate how much wax I'll need:

One 8 oz jar = 7.5 oz Net Weight (the contents of the jar weigh 7.5 oz)

I want to make four (4) of them so the story continues like this:

4 jars x 7.5 oz of wax in each container = 30 oz of wax needed for this project.

So, I get my big, fat Zak bowl out, place it on my scale, and tare it out so that it gives me a reading of only the contents that I measure into the bowl (in this case the 30 oz of wax).

I'm using a wax that's capable of holding 3-10% fragrance oil without problems. I think I'll go with 7% fragrance oil for this example. So, the story continues as follows:

30 ounces of wax x .07 = 2.1 ounces of fragrance oil

So, in summary, to make this batch of 4 candles I will use 30 ounces of wax and 2.1 ounces of fragrance oil.

Now what? You've got your work space set up, supplies out,

plan or "recipe" mapped out that includes how much wax and oil you'll need. Let's keep going...

Chapter 13: Preparing Glass Containers for Pouring (this will not apply to all containers such as metal tins)

Many problems people run into while making glass container candles can often be avoided by simply washing the containers they intend to use. A clean, dry jar at room temperature will provide you with the best opportunity for success.

In our business we looked at running all of our jars through a dishwasher as a last resort attempt to solve our jar issues that plagued us (wet spots or adhesions issues mainly). We were trying to avoid additional work for the thousands of jars we were preparing and the thought of having to run that many jars through the dishwasher was something I didn't even want to consider! Alas, we eventually got desperate enough (or smart enough, whatever) to give it a shot and a beam of sunshine emerged as a result. We have never looked back and literally have a room where all of our jars are received and run through the dishwasher before they're brought into the production area to be wicked and poured. I can't express enough how many headaches this has relieved. You're welcome.

A side note: if you're wondering (or stubborn like me) if you can get away with just wiping the jars out or hand-washing them, maybe you can and maybe you can't. Here's my experience for what it's worth:

Wiped jars with a microfiber cloth and rubbing alcohol, but the results showed significant streaking and sort of cloudy-like residue that was left in the jar. The jars looked spotless when wiped with the cloth/alcohol, but after being poured and given time to set up the streaks and cloudiness appeared. (wish I would've taken pictures!)

Washed jars by hand in hot water, small amount of regular dish soap, rinsed, and allowed to dry overnight. This resulted in a little bit better outcome than the alcohol wipe, but still showed streaking and slight cloudiness to the point we needed another solution.

As a last resort we ran the jars through the dishwasher... bingo! Success! This is what we do now with our clear glass containers. Our girl-Friday, Polly, is our girl on the dishwasher and we're ever so grateful to her!

Chapter 14: Set Up Your Jars to Be Poured

This is going to assume you're starting out with clean, dry jars and are ready to proceed with wicking them.

Affix wicks into each jar and then set the jars out where you will pour them. Here's a great link to an illustrated example of how to do this: How to affix wicks in Containers

Basically, cut a drinking straw to a length that accommodates the length of your wick and allows you to hold it, dip the wick clip into your glue pot, and then center and affix the wick to the bottom of the jar. Then you can just slip the drinking straw up and out of the jar leaving the wick in the jar.

TIP: Again, you don't need a fancy appliance to affix wicks in your containers. A regular drinking straw will do nicely!

Then you can set your jars out on a level surface where you will be able to easily pour the wax into them. I like to line mine up in a row with about 3-4 inches in-between each jar. Then I have enough room to come back and put the wick holders on the tops so the wick is held up nice and straight while they cool.

Chapter 15: Melting the Wax

So, again, this method is specific to what we do in our business. Candle making is kind of like raising kids: there's a lot of right ways to do it. Here's where things start to get interesting, tho!

You want to slowly melt the wax to a temperature of 185 degrees give or take a few degrees. Whether you use a Presto Pot or commercial melter, you simply load the wax and turn it on in the device you're using. Place a thermometer in the wax to monitor the temperature while it melts. Vegetable waxes can scorch and burn, so melt the wax slowly and monitor the temperature constantly. Once the wax starts melting you can turn up the temperature gradually until you reach the target temperature of 185 degrees. The wax can start to degrade if allowed to reach temperatures of 200 degrees and above, especially if held there for extended periods of time.

So, for example, this is what I do in our business: I load our big wax melter (Penny) with about 50 pounds of wax at a time, turn on the melter and set the temperature to 150 degrees. I come back and check it about an hour later and increase the temperature to my target temperature that I'll be working with (185 degrees usually).

Another example if you're using a Presto-Pot (which holds about 4 pounds of wax and we still use in our business for smaller jobs), I dump the measured wax into the Presto-Pot and turn it on. I set the temperature dial on the device so that it's well under the 200 degree mark. I hook a thermometer to the side of the pot to monitor the temperature while the wax melts and keep a close eye on it. It's too easy to have wax melt and temperatures soar well above 200 degrees even when the device has a temperature control unit. These Presto Pots don't have a very precise thermostat, so just be cautious. There's an alert function on our thermometer, too, and sometimes I'll set this to 185 and let the wax melt slowly while I tend to something else. The alarm will then sound when the wax reaches the correct temperature. You don't have to have a fancy thermometer with an alarm as long as you watch closely.

TIP: Just a reminder! Wax held at high temperatures (200+) for extended periods of time can scorch, burn, discolor, or otherwise degrade. In other words - money down the drain, my friends. You don't want this. Just allow yourself plenty of time, follow your road map, and work slowly to avoid the problem all together.

Chapter 16: Adding the Fragrance Oils

Once your wax has melted and the temperature is at least 185 degrees (but no higher than 190 or so) you add the fragrance oil. First, carefully pour the melted wax into your pouring pitcher and clip your thermometer to the side of the pouring pitcher. Next, add the pre-measured fragrance oil to the wax. Lastly, stir for two full minutes with a wooden spoon or, my favorite, a paint stir stick!

TIP: This sounds silly, but believe me when I say you will avoid a number of frustrating problems by stirring each batch for a FULL TWO (2) MINUTES (sorry to shout). This is worth an entire e-book on its own. Hell, it's worth its own banner across Main Street! All fragrance oils have different flash points and components. Some are harder to incorporate into the wax than others. Part of this has to do with flash points and part of it was explained to me but was completely over my head and I'd have to refer you to the scientist I reached out to at Elevance when I was having difficulties with our wax for further help in explaining it. The bottomline is adequate stirring. Just do it, I promise it's worth it. Two full minutes.

Chapter 17: Pouring the Candles

Once you have added the fragrance oils and stirred your batch for two full minutes you'll notice the temperature of the wax has decreased by 10-20 degrees and that's fine. Once the temperature of the wax has cooled to between 165-175 you can then pour the wax into your jars.

If you dink around and don't get the wax poured while it's between 165-175 degrees you may run into problems like poor glass adhesion, bumpy tops, and maybe even sinkholes. I used to think the cooler the pour temperature the better, but this hasn't held true for me.

TIP: When pouring the wax into the jars do it slowly, but purposefully. Pouring should be even, smooth, and without splashes and air bubbles. It takes time to get your hand at this, so grab some paper towels and embrace it! With smaller batches like we provide in our Recipes section you shouldn't have many problems with this. It's when you start pouring 4 pounds of wax out of your pitcher that things start getting dicey!

TIP: Smooth pouring will help you achieve a good adhesion of the wax to the glass container when the candles have cooled.

Chapter 18: Centering & Setting the Wicks, Curing the Candles, Removing Wick Bars, and Trimming Wicks

Once the candles have been poured, you'll want to place some sort of wick holder in place to hold the wick securely at the top while the candles set up. We use the metal wick bars available at CandleScience for this. I've tried using plain old wooden clothes pins and they work great, too! As long as you can center the wick (and keep it straight and taut) while the candle is setting up that's the main thing here.

Let your candles set up for a few hours at least before you try moving them or removing the wick bars. Ideally it's best to just leave them overnight (or a good 24 hours) in your work space before you try doing anything else with them at this point.

Once the candles have set up for 24 hours it's safe to remove the wick bars and trim the wicks to ¼". This is the time to take a paper towel or microfiber cloth (my favorite) to clean the jars of any wax drips or spills that occurred while pouring.

Chapter 19: Safety & Burn Testing

Make sure you let the candles set or "cure" as some call it for a minimum of 72 hours before test burning. There's some cool science at work during this time even if you can't detect anything with your eyes!

When I perform a burn test I am looking to see how the wax/wick/fragrance combination works together. I'm looking to see how long it takes to establish a full melt pool of the entire diameter of the candle. I also want to see how the wick performs. Is it small and compact, large and smoking, or is it just right?

I'm also testing the scent quality both as a cold, unlit candle (cold throw) as well as a hot, burning candle (hot throw). Sometimes I've loved a scent SO much upon the first impression (cold throw), but once it's lit and burning it's awful. Our first attempt at a true, citrusy orange scented candle had a beautiful, delicious cold-throw, but when it was burning it smelled like fuel! It was a disaster. Okay, you get the point, now let's get to it.

Here's How to Perform a Test Burn:
I'm test burning candles as I sit here and write this today! Truth is, I'm testing regularly. It takes a significant amount of time to test every container, scent, wax, and fragrance combo. I just consider it one part of our ever-changing, growing business.

There are many resources to help guide you through

test-burning a candle and I'll include some helpful links for you, but here's what I do:

Have a notebook dedicated specifically for burn testing your candles.

Set your candle on a flat surface free from any drafts.

Trim the wick to ¼".

Light your candle.

Do not leave candle unattended during the burn test!

Let candle burn until it achieves a full melt pool all the way to the edges of the container and ideally melts to a depth of about ¼". (a good candle will burn approximately one hour per inch of diameter to achieve a full melt pool)

Do not burn for more than 3-4 hours at a time.

You're shooting for candle to burn about 1 hour per inch of diameter of the candle to achieve the ideal full melt pool and melt depth (for example we burn our 8 oz straight sided jar no more than 3 hours when testing as the diameter is 2.25").

Watch the candle burning and keep notes about the performance. For example, if you light a candle with a 2.5" diameter and notice that it reaches a full melt pool and ¼" depth one hour into the test you probably have too large of a wick in the jar. Likewise, if you light this same candle and let it burn for 3 hours and you only have about half of a melt pool across the top of the candle your wick is likely too small.

At the end of the test burn, blow the candle out and make notes about performance and appearance of the candle. Let the candle sit for at least 7 hours (preferably overnight) and then run this test again with the same candle.

I would encourage and advise that you test your candles all the way through. The performance may change dramatically halfway through your test burn. You simply can't make a solid decision on an appropriate container/wax/fragrance/wick combo unless you see the test all the way through.

To read more in-depth on testing and how to perform a test burn here's a resource that helped me: test burning a candle (they also have a variety of videos on Youtube that you might find helpful - just enter "test burning a candle" in the search)

Chapter 20: Legal Stuff

I'll keep this really short here as I am clearly NOT a legal expert and am not qualified to give any sort of legal advice. Be prudent and do your homework. Operating out of your home? Talk to your insurance company. Intending to operate as a business with a particular declared legal structure? Talk to your insurance company. Don't have an insurance company? It's good to seek this service out to see what your insurance needs are exactly. Any reputable insurance company will provide you with this information free of charge.

Chapter 21: Safety Labels

You must label your product with safety information if you're going to sell to the public. You can find up-to-date labeling information and requirements specific to candles at the U.S. Consumer Product Safety Commission. Please consult with your insurance company and/or legal professionals to determine your requirements for where you live if you are pursuing a business or even just providing your goods to others as a hobby. Educate yourself on the liability issues that exist. Again, I'm not a legal professional and am not in any way providing legal advice on this issue.

Chapter 22: Troubleshooting: Sinkholes, Wet Spots, Candle Smokes when Lit, Candle Not Achieving Full Melt Pool, Fragrance Oil Problems, Inconsistent Results with Wax

This is a pretty good section for troubles you might encounter, but it's not all-inclusive. Just a reminder, this is specific to soy container candle making. I'm listing here the top issues we struggled with in our business using the C-3 Soy Nature Wax from www.Cierra Candles.com and the various fragrance oils from www.CandleScience.com. If you don't see your particular problem listed here, reach out to me and I'll be happy to help you if I can. Chances are I have encountered the same problem.

Also, when searching for answers for your own candle making woes please seek out credible sources to help you. Examples of credible sources would be the wax manufacturer and the wax supplier. Be very careful of advice you come across from "experts" in various forums all over the internet. You can usually tell who is worth listening to and who's not by the information they post. Just use your head. Stay away from myths and old wives tales when tackling your trouble shooting!

Problem: Sinkholes

Possible Causes: Room temperature too warm for the container used. Candle cooled too slowly as a result.

Try This: Try a cooler room when you pour the candles. For the 8 oz straight-sided jar we use in our business we keep the room around 65-70 degrees. For our 16 oz straight-sided jar we keep the room even lower at about 50-60 degrees.

Problem: Wet spots

Possible Causes: Too much fragrance oil used, containers too cold when pouring the wax in, jars are not clean, candles cooled too quickly, you didn't hold your tongue just right (just kidding)(sort of!)

Try This: Pour candles in a room that is around 60-70 degrees and will remain at that temp for at least 24 hours after you have poured the candles. The "wet spots" are actually places where the wax did not achieve full adhesion to the jar. There is no moisture involved. Be sure the containers are clean, dry, and at room temperature. You may need to lower the percentage of the oil you're using (try backing off on the amount by 1% and try again). There are some oils that give us chronic grief in this area and other oils that never seem to contribute to this problem at all. You'll just have to test and test some more until you find what works. We still have problems in this area at times, but I can usually nail it down by looking closely at the details.

Problem: Candle smokes when lit

Possible Causes: Oil content is too high, oil not fully incorporated in the wax, wick is too big, candle has been burning too long, or has been burning in a drafty area.

Try This: *Just remember any candle can (and usually will) smoke if in a drafty area. Also, you might decrease the amount of oil used (keep notes!); make sure to stir oil into the wax for at least two full minutes before pouring the wax into the containers; try a smaller wick; make sure the wick is always trimmed to ¼" before lighting; burn candles no longer than 2-3 hours at a time depending on the size of the container (generally, burn a candle 1 hour per inch of diameter of your container)

Problem: Candle Not Achieving Full Melt Pool

Possible Causes: Wick is too small for container, wrong wax for the application, candle isn't being burned properly

Try This: Choose a wick a size larger and test it; make sure you have chosen a wax specifically for containers rather than a pillar blend which has a higher melting point and will not melt as easily in a container application. Also, be sure to test burn a candle all the way through before you judge a wick to be too small.

Problem: Fragrance oil separates from the wax or settles on top of the candle

Possible Causes: Wax and oil not compatible, too much oil used, oil not stirred long enough to fully incorporate into the wax

Try This: Be sure to choose a fragrance oil specifically formulated to perform in soy wax; lower the percentage of oil you use in your recipe and be sure to add the oil at the correct temperature per the manufacturer; stir the oil in for two minutes or until you no longer see any sign of separation of the oil and the wax.

Problem: Inconsistent results with a wax you have used successfully in the past

Possible Causes: Wax "memory" may be at play here and/or excessive air was incorporated into the wax at the time of manufacturing. Crazy, I know, I had a hard time wrapping my head around this one, but I tried the solutions suggested to me by the manufacturer and I can't recall having this problem since.

Try This: Heat your wax up to 160-165 degrees and hold it at that temperature for 20 minutes then try working with it again. Soy wax has a "memory" (words of the manufacturer, not mine) that may need to be "erased" before you can work with it. I consider this standard operating procedure now when I am working with a new batch of wax. Be careful, though. Holding wax at high temperatures for long periods of time may compromise the wax (mainly causing it to discolor). Read all you can about your particular wax from your supplier as well as the manufacturer.

Chapter 23: RECIPES: Lavender 4 Oz Travel Tin Candles & Apple Harvest 8 Oz Straight-Sided Jar Candles

Below are a couple of our tried and true recipes we've used in our own business for a number of years now. This is a great starting point to start playing around with your own recipes! If you have questions, reach out to me and I'll try to help you along!

Lavender Travel Tin Soy Candles (yields eight (8) 4oz candles)

This is a classic Lavender scent and these travel tins are a perfect first-time project! These tins are really hard to screw up and not nearly as fussy as some of the larger glass jar containers can be. Perfect for gifting, stocking stuffers, fundraisers, etc. Want to see these in action in the real world? Here they are: Lavender Travel Tin Soy Candles

Cost: Approximate cost for the actual supplies for this "recipe" (not the equipment) is $25-30, but will leave you with some leftover tins, wicks, wax, and warning labels. The cost of the equipment will be about $60 or so. Not bad for a small startup, right?

Equipment & Supplies (links for specific items in resource section):

Presto Pot
Glue pot & glue pellets
Aluminum Pouring Pitcher
Eight (8) 4oz candle tins
27 ounces of C-3 wax
Pre-tabbed Eco 10 Wicks
1.85 oz (7% usage) of Lavender Fragrance Oil
Candle safety warning labels

Instructions:
Refer to previous sections on preparing work space, preparing containers, placing wicks in the containers, etc.

Melt wax to 185 degrees then add oil and be sure to stir for a full two minutes.

When wax has cooled to 165-175 degrees you can then pour into the containers. Pour up to the fill line indicated under the rim of the container.

Center wicks and secure each wick with a wick bar or wooden clothespin to hold in place until candle has set.

Allow to set for at least 4 hours or longer before removing wick bars.

Trim wicks and place lids on candles.

Clean containers of any wax spills.

Affix candle warning sticker on bottom of candles.

TIP: Just a quick note about this recipe! I have a near perfect track record with this recipe as long as I pour while the wax is above 160 degrees. If you're using a high-melt commercial glue to secure your wicks in the container you can get away with pouring immediately after you mix the oil into the wax.

TIP: If you're using a standard "glue gun" glue from the craft store you may have to let the wax cool some (below 160 degrees maybe) prior to pouring or you'll risk the glue being melted and the wick detaching from the container due to the heat! Ask me how I know (ha!) Just experiment with what you have and you'll find out quickly what will work for your own needs.

Apple Harvest 8 oz Straight-Sided Jar Candles (yields 4 candles)

This is seriously one of my favorites! We've been making this one since the very beginning and it has been a top seller each fall. This size of container is also our top selling size, too. I hope you love it! See it in real life here: Apple Cider Petite Jar Candle

Cost: Approximate cost for the actual supplies for this "recipe" (not the equipment) is $25-30, but will leave you with some leftover tins, wicks, wax, and warning labels. The cost of the equipment will be about $60 or so.

Equipment & Supplies:

Presto Pot
Glue pot & glue pellets
Aluminum Pouring Pitcher
Four (4) 8 oz Jars
Four (4) Lids to fit jars
30 ounces of C-3 wax
Eco 12 Wicks
2.1 oz (7% usage) of Apple Harvest Fragrance Oil
Candle safety warning labels

Instructions:
Refer to previous sections on preparing work space, preparing containers, placing wicks in the containers, etc.

Be sure room temperature is between 60-70 degrees.

Melt wax to 185 degrees then add oil and be sure to stir for a full two minutes.

When wax has cooled to between 160-170 degrees you can then pour into the jars. Pour up to the "shoulder" of the container, but stop before you reach the "neck" of the container.

Center wicks and secure each wick with a wick bar or wooden clothespin to hold in place until candle has set.

Allow to set for at least 8 hours or longer before removing wick bars.

Trim wicks and place lids on candles.

Affix candle warning sticker on bottom of candles.

Chapter 24: Resources & Suppliers

I've mentioned them throughout this candle making guide, but here they are in list form for your convenience!

C-3 Wax:
Cierra Candles in Washington State
CandleMakingSupplies.Net in California

TIP: To state the obvious (which I, of course, had to learn the hard way) it's best to order supplies from the suppliers closest to you when you start ordering in larger quantities. (Did I mention the first time I tried to order a 50 pound box of wax from North Carolina?)

TIP: Type "candle making supplies" into your favorite search engine and you'll quickly find suppliers in your neck of the woods.

Fragrance Oils:
CandleScience
Peak Candle Supplies
Cierra Candles

TIP: There are so, so many suppliers selling fragrance oils. It's hard to tell who has good quality oils and who doesn't. Test, test, test and make your own determination always.

General Candle Making Equipment:
CandleScience
Cierra Candles
Peak Candle Supply

Containers:
CandleScience
SKS Bottle & Packaging

Equipment & Supplies for the Recipes in this Book:

Lavender Travel Tin Soy Candles:

Presto Pot
https://www.amazon.com/Presto-114324-Kitchen-Kettle-Multi-Cooker/dp/B00006IUWH

Glue Pot & Pellets
http://www.commercial-hot-glue.com/shop/page/product_detail/Product/ca4c96721c0cd46e3a645699ed18ac42.html

Aluminum Pouring Pitcher
https://www.candlescience.com/equipment/pouring-pitcher

Eight (8) 4oz candle tins

https://www.candlescience.com/containers/4oz-candle-tin

27 Ounces of C-3 Wax
https://www.candlescience.com/containers/4oz-candle-tinc3 wax
cierra candles

Pre-tabbed Eco 10 Wicks
https://www.candlescience.com/wick/eco-10

1.85 oz (7% usage) of Lavender Fragrance Oil
https://www.candlescience.com/fragrance/lavender-fragrance-oil

Candle Safety Warning Labels
https://www.candlescience.com/equipment/1inch-labels

Apple Harvest 8 oz Straight-Sided Jar Candles:

Presto Pot
https://www.amazon.com/Presto-114324-Kitchen-Kettle-Multi-Co
oker/dp/B00006IUWH

Glue Pot & Pellets
http://www.commercial-hot-glue.com/shop/page/product_detail/P
roduct/ca4c96721c0cd46e3a645699ed18ac42.html

Aluminum Pouring Pitcher
https://www.candlescience.com/equipment/pouring-pitcher

Four (4) 8 Ounce Straight-sided Jars
https://www.candlescience.com/containers/medium-straight-side

d-jar

Four (4) Lids to Fit Straight-Sided Jars
https://www.candlescience.com/containers/70-silver-twist-top

27 Ounces of C-3 Wax
https://www.candlescience.com/containers/4oz-candle-tinc3 wax
cierra candles

Pre-tabbed Eco 12 Wicks
https://www.candlescience.com/wick/eco-12

2.1 oz (7% usage) of Apple Harvest Fragrance Oil
https://www.candlescience.com/fragrance/apple-harvest-fragran
ce-oil

Candle Safety Warning Labels
https://www.candlescience.com/equipment/1inch-labels

Here's a great resource for test burning your candles:

How to Test Burn a Candle - Candle Science

Chapter 25: Wrap it up! I guess this is where we part... or is it?

Whew! We made it! So, that's kind of the gist of the whole operation, but please know that even with all of this information placed into action and followed precisely without any errors may result in an occasional blooper. If that's the case I may suggest that you didn't hold your tongue right while pouring the candles or some nonsense. It happens. But, I promise the recipes provided will be the best place to start and actually find consistent results and then you can start experimenting with your own fragrance oils and containers and maybe even a different wax if you're brave enough! You can do it!

Like I mentioned fifty times previously, this was my first stab at getting some usable, reliable information out there on Container Soy Candle making. I hope it's been useful to you! I'd love your feedback and honest review on Amazon. Please take the time to do this and help make this a better product for all users.

Want to be the first to see new publications as they roll out? Sign up for our newsletter on our contact page at http://www.aggiesonmain.com

Want to see our little business in action? Check us out at http://www.aggiesonmain.com or see back stage happenings on Instagram @aggiesonmain

Lastly, if you have any helpful comments, honest critiques, or just want to connect please feel free to reach out to me at aggiesonmain@gmail.com

About the Author

Ok, so Lisa is obviously not an author. Please cut her a break if you found this publication to be completely worthless and are headed straight to Amazon to leave a sting of a review. Please consider the intent of this effort and understand that the point of the publication was to share information so that others may have a leg up in this handmade business world. If you have an idea to make this better, she'd love to hear from you!

Lisa is an Oregon native, wishes she could be on assignment for NatGeo, has a semi-serious love-hate relationship with politics, has only herself to blame for her feisty daughter, and somehow managed to marry the most precious-hearted man there ever was. She loves dogs, too. Her dogs. This might crack you up, too: her first business was sewing her mom's old wash cloths into small purses and trying to sell them to her elementary school classmates who never had any damn money. Oh, and she's funny. Just ask her little boy crush, Cash.

Made in the USA
Columbia, SC
11 April 2018